THE CHURCH WILL NOT GO THROUGH THE TRIBULATION

S. Franklin Logsdon

REGULAR BAPTIST PRESS
1300 North Meacham Road
Post Office Box 95500
Schaumburg, Illinois 60195

© 1980
1982-Second Printing

Regular Baptist Press
Schaumburg, Illinois
All Rights Reserved

The Church Will Not Go Through the Tribulation

A fearful, indescribable, calamitous, unprecedented holocaust will befall this sinful world. It is termed the *tribulation period* or the *seventieth week of Daniel.* Some believe the Church will go through it. Others hold that the Church will go halfway through. Still others maintain that the Church will not so much as enter it. These people are referred to, respectively, as posttribulationists, midtribulationists and pretribulationists.

For God's people to be divided in any area of divine truth is regrettable, but such is the case in this instance. It is not, however, sufficient cause for ill feeling, unpleasant argumentation and broken fellowship. Some of our cherished friends and admirable colleagues in the ministry hold an opposite view of this matter without affecting the flow of Christian affection. And that is as it should be. But since each must be persuaded in his own mind, and since it is perfectly natural for one to express one's convictions, we present the following treatise for prayerful consideration.

We suggest the simplest possible approach to this profound matter—just three terse questions: (1) What is the Great Tribulation? (2) Why is there controversy? (3) How may one determine the truth of the matter?

What Is the Great Tribulation?

First, the Tribulation cannot be equated with any period or set of circumstances in the past. In the January 1980 issue of *Christian Life* magazine, a full-page advertisement of a new book entitled *The Church Will Go Through the Tribula-*

tion appeared. The main sales pitch was that in times past God did not remove His people from trials, but allowed them to go through them victoriously.

It is clear in this instance, as well as in many others, that posttribulationists do not distinguish between the problems, sorrows and afflictions common to mankind and the Great Tribulation prophesied to come. Every believer knows that God said in Job 5:7, "Man is born unto trouble, as the sparks fly upward." Every believer knows that Jesus said, "In the world ye shall have tribulation" (John 16:33). Every believer knows that Paul explained, "Our light affliction, which is but for a moment, worketh for us a far more exceeding and eternal weight of glory" (2 Cor. 4:17). Every believer knows that Peter warned, "Think it not strange concerning the fiery trial . . . which cometh upon you . . ." (1 Pet. 4:12, ASV). God does give His people sufficient grace. But why can we not believe the Lord Jesus when He emphasized, "For *then* shall be great tribulation, *such as was not since the beginning of the world to this time, no, nor ever shall be*" (Matt. 24:21; *emphasis mine*). This is what we are discussing. And this period of unprecedented hardship was *never* decreed for the Church.

To facilitate a clearer understanding, we advance five words: *definition, designations, descriptions, devastations, duration*. A comprehension of the collective connotations involved in these words should be enlightening to any open mind.

Definition. The tribulation period is the final seven years of God's determined dealings with Daniel's people and the holy city, to finish Israel's transgression, to end Israel's sins and to make reconciliation for Israel's iniquity (Dan. 9:24).

Designations. Such expressive terms are given as "the day of the LORD"(Amos 5:18); the "time of Jacob's trouble" (Jer. 30:7); "the wrath is come" (1 Thess. 2:16); "the great day of his wrath" (Rev. 6:17); "wrath of Almighty God" (Rev. 19:15); "the indignation of the LORD" (Isa. 34:2); and "the hour of temptation" (Rev. 3:10).

Descriptions. "Woe unto you that desire the day of the LORD! to what end is it for you? the day of the LORD is darkness, and not light. As if a man did flee from a lion, and a bear met him; or went into the house, and leaned his hand on the wall, and a serpent bit him. Shall not the day of the LORD be darkness, and not light? even very dark, and no brightness in it?" (Amos 5:18-20; see also Zech. 14:12; Rev. 16:18-20).

Exclamations such as the following have echoed down the corridors of time concerning the fearful woes which will characterize this time of outpoured wrath:

> What an experience for man is bound up in their awful brevity!
> What plagues descend with that sharp sickle!
> What a crash comes as it alights upon a world dead ripe for judgment!
> What powers and systems fall before it!
> What agonies it brings to them who bear the mark of the beast!
> What cries and thunders and lightnings and earthquakes and hailstones and trembling it arouses!
> It includes all the disasters manifested in the bowls of wrath!
> It sinks all the riches and glories of a godless world into one common ruin never to be brought up again.
> It is the sorrowful sweeping away forever of that which the Scriptures describe as the termination of the whole present order of things.

Devastations. The cosmic upheavals, to say nothing of the fierce heavenly disturbances, will be so terrifyingly horrendous as to place them beyond human comprehension. They will consist of seven seal judgments, seven trumpet judgments and seven vial or bowl judgments. These are not exactly consecutive in development; neither are they concurrent. Someone has aptly said, "Imagine yourself looking through a telescope which has three adjustments. You look as far as you can through the first adjustment, then you move it to the second, then to the third. In each instance you are looking in the same direction but seeing farther and more clearly with each adjustment." So it is with these judgments. Each one is a greater magnification of the fierceness of divine wrath.

With the breaking of the first seal, the terrifying beast (Antichrist) makes a mad dash to conquer the world with no regard for human life (Rev. 6:2). Then peace is taken from the earth (Rev. 6:4), famine ensues (Rev. 6:6) and death and hell hold sway (Rev. 6:8). Matters grow progressively worse as the world's worst dictator seeks to consolidate and to further his position; and when he does, the earth will writhe in misery and woe. But it is not only a reign of human terror, it is also a time of divine wrath outpoured (Rev. 6:17). These judgments will drape this sin-sick earth with the blackest, fiercest, bitterest plagues ever. There will be a total revocation of civil rights. And this is but an intimation of what it is all about. The descriptions and devastations pertain largely to the second half of the week.

Duration. The chronometric measurement is irrefutable. It is mathematically calculated. God determined seventy weeks of years in His dealings with Israel (Dan. 9:24). These were divided into three categories; namely, seven weeks of years until the walls were built about Jerusalem and sixty-two weeks of years until Messiah was cut off. These add up to sixty-nine weeks, and sixty-nine subtracted from seventy leaves one week of years. This is what is in view here. This one week is divided into two equal parts, and each of these two parts is described as forty-two months, twelve hundred and sixty days; or time, times and half time. The first half of the week is termed *the Tribulation*; the second half, *the Great Tribulation*.

The division is pinpointed. It will take place when the beast, the Antichrist, sets up his image, "the abomination of desolation," in the temple (Matt. 24:15). This marks the middle of the week.

Referring to the second half of the week, the Great Tribulation, Jesus said: "And except those days should be shortened, there should no flesh be saved: but for the elect's sake those days shall be shortened" (Matt. 24:22). Because of this assertion, some people are of the impression that there will be fewer days in the second half of the week than in the first. This cannot be. It would not only contradict a definite statement of Scripture, but would render incorrect the period of ministry for the two witnesses, about whom it is said, ". . . And they shall prophesy a thousand two hundred and threescore days . . ." (Rev. 11:3). As Revelation 13:5 says, ". . . Power was given unto him [the beast] to continue forty and two months."

How then may we understand what Jesus meant by ". . . except those days should be shortened"? Simply by inquiring about the meaning of the word *days*. In Genesis 1:5 we read, "And God called the light Day, and the darkness he called Night." Thus, it is the light periods which will be shortened. Here we may ask, Why? How?

The reason is clear. The fourth angel will pour out his vial on the sun and men will be scorched (Rev. 16:8, 9); that is, the sun will become a *nova*. A nova is a star, or heavenly body, that suddenly increases its light output tremendously. The resultant misery will be unspeakable, so the light periods will be shortened during those days.

How? From the human viewpoint, it could only result from God causing the earth to revolve more rapidly on its axis or by moving the earth out of its present position. The former suggestion is untenable, for then no flesh could survive. The latter suggestion is not only the likely one but the divinely revealed one. "Therefore I will shake the heavens, and the earth shall remove out of her place, in the wrath of the LORD of hosts, and in the day of his fierce anger" (Isa. 13:13). This will curtail the daylight period.

Why Is There Controversy?

Were we to seek basic reasons for the prevailing unhealthy division among God's people in this most critical of all hours and on this most blessed of all doctrines, the glorious appearing of our blessed Lord, we would be forced sooner or later to concede that dispensational misunderstanding heads the list.

By and large our posttribulational friends claim not to be dispensationalists; that is, they reject the so-called dispensational approach to Bible revelation. And here, of course, there is also misunderstanding, for they are indeed dispensationalists if they are preaching the gospel of the grace of God. All of my close posttribulationist acquaintances do preach the gospel with compassion and compulsion. They may not, however, appreciate or employ the term *dispensational*. Who would object if they preferred the word *era* or *age*? One thing is certain. No servant of Christ is true to his commission if he takes his audiences back under the Levitical ceremonial procedure or back under John the Baptist's message.

Augustine (354-430) said, "Distinguish the times and you will harmonize Scripture." This presupposes that God has order and arrangement in His "purpose that is purposed upon the whole earth" (Isa. 14:26). Thus, we are bound to admit to a number of irrefutable Bible facts.

1. That God Himself divided or departmentalized the human family (Gen. 10:32); that He chose Israel in a special sense (Deut. 7:6); that He is calling out a distinct company known as the Church (Acts 15:14); that He in this present age recognizes the divisions He has made (1 Cor. 10:32).

2. That God, having so differentiated among men, has different and distinct dealings with them; that He made covenants with Israel to which Gentiles are strangers (Eph. 2:12); that He makes promises to the Church which others cannot claim (Rom. 8:17).

3. That differences of divine dealing presage differences of destination and reward; that the Church will appear "with him in glory" (Col. 3:4); that saved Israel will appear with Him in the land promised to Abraham (Ezek. 37:12, 21).

4. That God Who made the nations both appointed the bounds of their habitation and determined their times (Acts 17:26).

5. That the differences of divine covenants and decrees are characterized by the time element in application and administration. There is initiation and termination, inception and conclusion, beginning and ending. As an illustration in point, we note that the "times of the Gentiles" had a definite starting point (Dan. 2:37) and will have a specific cessation (Dan. 2:34).

6. That there must follow the fact that the Church, likewise, had a specific commencement (Acts 2) and will have a specific consummation (1 Thess. 4:16, 17).

7. That the Church is separate and distinct from Israel in position, privilege and prospect; that the time period of God's dealings with it does not coincide with or overlap the period of His dealings with Israel; that, therefore, it must follow that we cannot exegete the Church either into Daniel's sixty-ninth week past or into Daniel's seventieth week future.

The problem of exegesis. This is the area of critical analysis. In presenting a clear, accurate picture of the Rapture, as indeed would hold true for any doctrine, important but simple laws of interpretative procedure must be respected. Pertinence is perhaps the most basic interpretive law. Are the references cited applicable? Is the subject at hand unquestionably in view in the context?

Those who keep on the right side of the cross will be more nearly correct in their conclusions and concepts regarding the Church, both as to its present and its future. To wander into the inapplicable can but precipitate confusion.

Those who insist that Matthew 24:27-31 is identical in meaning with 1 Thessalonians 4:16 and 17 would do well to set the two portions down in juxtaposition. In this way the contrast becomes evident; and this being true, the Matthew context cannot be used as proof that the Church will go through the Great Tribulation.

Matthew 24:27-31	1 Thessalonians 4:16, 17
Signs in the skies (v. 27)	No such signs mentioned
Armageddon in view (v. 28)	Armageddon not in view
Disruptions in the heavens (v. 29)	Tribulation not indicated
Signs of second advent (v. 30)	A reunion in the heavens
People on earth mourn (v. 30)	Joy in meeting the Lord
Son of man comes in clouds (v. 30)	Saints go up in clouds
	Christ Himself descends
Christ sends His angels (v. 31)	Christ descends with trump of God
Angels sound trumpets (v. 31)	
Angels gather His elect (v. 31)	Christ catches up His saints
No resurrection mentioned	Dead in Christ are raised

Confusion of terminology and type. We are fettered with religious cliches, meaningless colloquialisms and traditional axioms. In the province of prophecy this is very apparent. For instance, what is meant by the oft-heard expression, "looking for the second coming of Christ"? There is a vast difference between looking for the "blessed hope" and looking for the second advent. Those who are looking for the second coming of Christ are expecting to go through the Great Tribulation. The first coming was His descent to this earth at Bethlehem. His second coming will be His descent to the Mount of Olives after the Great Tribulation.

To state that the second coming is in two phases—Christ coming for His saints, then later coming with His saints—is not a satisfactory or true explanation. Christ came the first time in one stage, and He will come the second time in one stage. Please observe that this is distinctly the fulfillment of Old Testament prophesies.

Observe, further, that while the Old Testament prophets saw these two towering mountain peaks, they did not see the valley of the Church Age in between, a matter "Which in other ages was not made known unto the sons of men, as it is now revealed unto his holy apostles and prophets by the Spirit" (Eph. 3:5).

There are certain Church exclusives, and one of these is the fact that the Lord, the Head of the Body (Col. 1:18), will appear in the heavens (not come to earth) to catch up (rapture) the members of His Body (1 Thess. 4:16). Then He will turn to His prophesied dealings with Daniel's people (Dan. 9:24). When He resumes His dealings with Israel, He will have completed His earthly dealings with His Church.

And when it comes to types, posttribulationists refer to Daniel in the lions' den and to the three Hebrews in the fiery furnace as illustrative of the Church being *kept* in the fierceness of the Great Tribulation. These references, of course, are clearly not applicable; hence, useless in this connection. These experiences were the vented animosity of the enemy against God's people. The plagues of the Great Tribulation are the wrath of God against His enemies, and those who cite the Church's martyrs to support posttribulation contention should know that they were the victims of satanic vengeance. The Great Tribulation will be the fearful judgment of God in unprecedented measure upon a world that rejected His Son.

On the other hand, the accounts of the Flood and the destruction of Sodom are quite apropos, simply because in each instance it was the judgment of God. Noah was spared from the Deluge (taken from the earth while the Flood persisted) as all others outside the ark perished. Lot had to be brought out of Sodom before the judgment could come, for God said, ". . . I cannot do any thing till thou be come thither" (Gen. 19:22). "Then the LORD rained upon Sodom and Gomorrah brimstone and fire. . . " (Gen. 19:24). It is difficult to believe that the Lord will be less mindful of and less compassionate for His own in this future time of His poured-out judgment.

In our day, when a nation declares war, it is customary to recall its ambassadors before hostilities begin. The tribulation judgments are a long prophesied war declared on this sinful and rebellious earth, and the Lord will recall His ambassadors (2 Cor. 5:20) before the fulfillment of this prophecy.

With Noah it was "Come in" (see Gen. 7:1); with Lot it was "Come out" (see Gen. 19:22); and with the Church it will be "Come up" (see 1 Thess. 4:16, 17).

In each instance God delivers His own from the judgment which He Himself imposes while unbelievers must experience what they are now laying up for themselves, ". . . wrath against the day of wrath and revelation of the righteous judgment of God" (Rom. 2:5).

Some attempt to explain the Rapture as a going out of the bride to meet the Bridegroom and her immediate return with Him. They believe the five wise virgins in Matthew 25:2 support this view. Here again is an obvious misapplication. Citing a plural figure of virgins as applicable to the Church not only puts the Church where it is not found, but it fails to harmonize with Paul's careful statement, ". . . I have espoused you to one husband that I may present you as a chaste virgin [singular] to Christ" (2 Cor. 11:2).

The problem of word meanings. We must differentiate between *wrath* and *condemnation* in Bible doctrine. When Paul wrote, ". . . Jesus, which delivered us [believers] from the wrath to come" (1 Thess. 1:10), he was not referring to the condemnation of an eternal hell but the fierceness of the Great Tribulation. The same is true in 1 Thessalonians 5:9: "For God hath not appointed us [Paul and all believers] to wrath, but to obtain salvation by our Lord Jesus Christ." What salvation shall those already saved from eternal condemnation receive? Salvation from the wrath of the Great Tribulation. Thus, the true believer is saved both from wrath and condemnation, for Jesus said, ". . . I also will keep thee from the hour of temptation" (Rev. 3:10), which is the Great Tribulation.

It is said that Saul of Tarsus, by mistreating the Church, was actually persecuting the Savior (Acts 9:5), for believers are one with Him—"members of his body, of his flesh, and of his bones" (Eph. 5:30). Since God has committed all judgment to His Son (John 5:22), Jesus will be the agent Who pours out the vials and plagues in that day. Since no one can escape the horrors of this universal chastening (Amos 5:19), if the Church is on the earth at that time, then by the same token He would be chastening Himself. This is not conceivable.

It may be asked why Jesus said, ". . . For the elect's sake

those days shall be shortened" (Matt. 24:22) if the Church will not be in the Great Tribulation. First, let it be said that it is difficult to comprehend how one can discover the Church in the context where this verse appears. Second, the word *elect* has a variety of applications. That which is elect has been divinely chosen. Priests were chosen of God (Deut. 21:5); judges were chosen (Judges 2:18); kings were chosen (1 Sam. 10:24); Israel was chosen (Deut. 7:6) and the Church is chosen (2 Thess. 2:13). The tribulation saints likewise will be chosen of God, the initial converts being termed the "firstfruits unto God and to the Lamb" (Rev. 14:4). It therefore seems unwise for people to argue for the Church's presence in Daniel's seventieth week on the strength of this statement in Matthew 24:22 in which Jesus speaks of the elect of a future time.

Perhaps a comment should be made concerning the *last trump.* ". . . We shall not all sleep, but we shall all be changed, in a moment, in the twinkling of an eye, at the last trump . . ." (1 Cor. 15:51, 52).

The *trump* is the sound or the blast; it is not the instrument itself. And the word *last* is connected with the sound, not the instrument. When the apostle refers to the trumpet, he very noticeably does not term it the last. Yet one prominent posttribulationist writer says, "The last trump means the last and is, therefore, the last of the seven trumpets of the Tribulation." Reason could not be dealt a more severe blow! Even if it were the last trump of the last trumpet in 1 Corinthians 15:52, that would not make it the seventh trumpet judgment, for the convincing reason that the wrath period is not even remotely associated with the context.

Trumpets in Bible days had various forms and a variety of uses. The trumpet concerning Israel had its own peculiar connotations. The trumpet in the Tribulation will have a separate importance. When our blessed Lord descends in the air, the significance of the trumpet is that of gathering His own people (the Church) unto Himself. The reason it is termed the "last trump" is that it is the final signal of the Captain of the Lord's hosts for this age. It terminates the Church's activities and heralds the glad day of meeting her Lord. It is not right to carry the thought beyond this and locate it in another area of unrelated Scripture.

The last trump of 1 Corinthians 15:52 is identical with the "trump of God" in 1 Thessalonians 4:16, and absolutely not synonymous with the seventh trumpet judgment of Revelation 11:15-19. In the former, the Lord receives His Church; in the latter, the kingdoms of the world. In the former, the Church is caught up; in the latter, the four and twenty elders fall on their faces. In the former, there is joy unspeakable; in the latter, thunderings, earthquake and great hail.

In the tribulation context of the Book of Revelation, we note the Jew and his temple, but never the Church and its leaders; the covenant of Antichrist with Israel, but no such official dealings of Antichrist with the Church. Noteworthy too is the fact that the seven lampstands of the Church (Rev. 1:13) give way to the two lampstands of the extraordinary witnesses (Rev. 11:4), both of whom are of Old Testament vintage.

Thus, by statement and symbol, by figure and fact, the Church is not discoverable in the seventieth week of Daniel, especially the second half—the Great Tribulation.

Repeatedly, we have found our posttribulationist brethren denouncing the "secret rapture" taught by the pretribulationists. Frankly, in more than fifty years of studying, preaching, teaching, authoring and associating with godly men, I have never once heard a pretribulationist use such an expression. Nor have I ever employed it myself.

However, it is not difficult to see how such an impression could be gained, for Paul said, "Behold, I shew you a mystery; we shall not all sleep, but we shall all be changed, in a moment, in the twinkling of an eye, . . ." (1 Cor. 15:51, 52). Scientists tell us that a twink, an involuntary flutter of the eyelid, takes place consistently in eleven-hundredths of a second. Such incomprehensible swiftness could well make the event unnoticeable to the unbelievers left behind. This leaves little room for argument. Choose your own term—secrecy or rapidity.

Some of our highly esteemed friends ask why the Church for thirteen hundred centuries did not teach the pretrib position, at least not with any prominence. Well, the fact is that there are many matters of present-day concern which were not emphasized in former times, chiefly because they were not relevant then.

The Holy Spirit came to guide us "into *all* truth" (John 16:13, *emphasis mine*), but not all of it at the same time. He does all things decently, and in order. He may withhold the emphasis of certain truth, or even its revelation, until the propitious moment. For instance, pursuant to our Lord's resurrection, He was asked, ". . . Wilt thou at this time restore again the kingdom to Israel?" His reply was, ". . . It is not for you to know [now] the times or the seasons, which the Father hath put in his own power" (Acts 1:6, 7). Jesus was simply saying that it was not at that moment necessary for them to become concerned about this particular fact.

Further, ". . . Christ also loved the church [from before the foundation of the world], and gave himself for it" (Eph. 5:25). Yet, Paul says concerning "the mystery," the Church, "Which in other ages was not made known unto the sons of men, as it is *now* revealed unto his holy apostles and prophets by the Spirit" (Eph. 3:5, *emphasis mine*).

Still further, it was not until the early part of the twentieth century that students of prophecy began emphasizing Russia's prophetic role; and, even later, the awakening of China, the sleeping giant; the alliance of Iran, Libya, Ethiopia, East Germany and Turkey with Russia in the upcoming invasion of Israel; the return of Israel to the land; the reconciliation of Islamic Egypt to Israel as Esau embraced Jacob after years of hostility; the fact that Jerusalem was becoming a cup of trembling to the whole world (Zech. 12:2, 3); and the European alliance of nations. These and many more matters of prophetic importance are end-time developments. The Spirit of God did not seem to impress earlier generations with such remote matters, events of no imminent significance. Thus, historical silence should not be called upon to invalidate a doctrine so currently clear.

Another matter prominently stressed by our posttribulationist friends is that of a Margaret MacDonald of Port Glasgow, Scotland, having a vision of believers being caught away. She is alleged to have communicated this dream to Pastor Edward Irving and his congregation of the Catholic Apostolic Church in London around 1830. This information is said to have been transmitted to Mr. James Nelson Darby, and through him, to Dr. C. I. Scofield. In due course, it flooded the Christian community.

Men of such stature, usefulness and credibility as J. N. Darby and Dr. C. I. Scofield were not so naive. They were eminently men of God who knew well how to go "To the law and to the testimony . . ." (Isa. 8:20), and how to search the Scriptures with the guidance of the Holy Spirit.

We could simplify matters greatly if we would stick to

the Scriptures. "My sheep hear my voice . . . ," the Lord Jesus emphasized. Nowhere are we instructed to consult the voice of history either to build or to blast a doctrine. We would not follow the voice of a Margaret MacDonald any more than we would follow the voice of a Joseph Smith. We are "fully furnished" in the Scriptures. Therefore, if it isn't in the Bible we don't want it. If it is in the Bible, we had better give heed to it!

Granted, a woman claimed to have had a vision of believers being caught up to be with the Lord. Granted, she revealed that vision to Pastor Edward Irving. Granted, her so-called vision bears some resemblance to the doctrine of the Rapture as we know it and believe it. We might revert to the vernacular and ask, "So what?" No one can stand in a court of justice and convince the judge and the jury that Margaret MacDonald influenced these Christian leaders. Yet, after one hundred fifty years, the attempt is being waged to discredit the credibility of these men of God who are not here to defend themselves.

It is unthinkable that Mr. Darby, who was so adamantly opposed to women teaching men, would follow the dream of a woman. It is equally inconsonant with reason to believe that a brilliant, godly man like Dr. Scofield, with his mind drilled in logic and skilled in weighing evidence as a former lawyer, and with his constant exhortation to rightly divide the Word of truth, would be influenced by a lone woman's visionary report, especially when he never so much as met her.

A booklet presenting the posttribulation argument was handed me recently. On the front cover is a cartoon showing two men pondering their Bibles. One man looks quite distressed, and the other man says to him, "Who said Rapture? Peter? No. Paul? Nah. James? Nope. John, had to be John! No. Jude? Never. Jesus? He did not!" This apparently was done with the utmost sincerity to be convincing and decisive, but it is pitifully illogical and utterly meaningless.

The weakest student of the Bible, if he wanted to wax sarcastic and to toy with divine truth, could substitute the Trinity, the Incarnation, expiation, pardon, atonement and many, many other precious doctrines. Did Peter, Paul, James, John, Jude or Jesus mention the words *trinity, incarnation, expiation* or *pardon*? Of course not, but each of these truths is eternally woven into the fabric of the Scriptures. Likewise, "caught up" in 1 Thessalonians 4:17 means "to be raptured" or "snatched away." The author of the booklet mentioned above says to his readers, "Look it up and see if you can find 'rapture.' It is not in the New Testament." Could he not as well ask, "See if you can find 'trinity,' 'incarnation' or 'expiation' "? Suffice it to state that the Rapture is definitely taught, and that it is "the blessed hope" for the believer. We are to meet the true Christ, not the Antichrist.

How May One Determine the Truth of the Matter?

Is there not some way in the midst of this unfortunate controversy for one to determine for oneself, with a degree of certainty, just what the Bible actually says about the matter? Well, I could ask Dr. So and So. But would I be sure Dr. So and So has an accurate appreciation of the subject? Or I could consult the best commentary. But which is the best commentary?

A neighbor inherited a fine collection of tools from a deceased friend. Being an office man all his working days, he had no perceptible aptitude for mechanical procedures. However, the tools were a challenge to his manhood and he began to putter around with them. Soon he became capable of performing minor repairs around the home and could construct items of a not-too-complicated character. His family was vocally pleased with his accomplishments.

Having a few tools with which to work and seeking the guidance of the Holy Spirit, any devoted, discerning, desiring Christian should arrive at some satisfying conclusion concerning the Church and its relation to the Great Tribulation. We offer the following tools for this undertaking. Or, perhaps we should call them tests.

The definition test. The Tribulation is defined as the final period in God's determined dealings with Daniel's people in order to finish Israel's transgression, to make an end of Israel's sins and to make reconciliation for Israel's iniquity. This is clearly stated in Daniel 9:24.

Surely we cannot see in this defined intention of the infinite God the presence and participation of the New Testament Church. The transgression which God intends to finish is Israel's long-standing rejection of the Messiah Whom He sent to them. However, after the Great Tribulation, Israel will acknowledge and receive her King. Here is the record: "I . . . will refine them as silver is refined, and will try them as gold is tried: they shall call on my name, and I will hear them: I will say, It is my people: and they shall say, The LORD is my God" (Zech. 13:9). The Church, of course, has already made this acknowledgment by faith and has received Him as Savior and Lord.

When God speaks about making an end of Israel's sins, He is referring specifically to their idolatry. When they were brought into covenant relationship with Him, they were explicitly exhorted, "Thou shalt have no other gods before me." Yet, as unbelievable as it is, we read in Jeremiah 7:18, "The children gather wood, and the fathers kindle the fire, and the women knead their dough, to make cakes to the queen of heaven, and to pour out drink offerings unto other gods, that they may provoke me to anger." They even engaged in the manufacture of idols, and the Lord warned them, saying, "Because Ephraim [Israel] hath made many altars to sin, altars shall be unto him to sin" (Hos. 8:11). "Turn ye unto him from whom the children of Israel have deeply revolted. For in that day every man shall cast away his idols of silver, and his idols of gold, which your own hands have made unto you for a sin" (Isa. 31:6, 7). Israel's history is sadly discolored with idolatry, but God will bring this to an end.

He will also "make reconciliation for iniquity." Iniquity is inward perversity, rebellion and persistent disobedience. It is no wonder Jeremiah wept over these ancient people. They brazenly informed him, "As for the word that thou hast spoken unto us in the name of the LORD, we will not hearken unto thee. But we will certainly do whatsoever thing goeth forth out of our own mouth, to burn incense unto the queen of heaven . . ." (Jer. 44:16, 17). When the chastening rod of Jacob's trouble is applied (in the Great Tribulation), two-thirds of the Jews will die, but one-third will be saved (Zech. 13:8). Then they will say, "Come, and let us return unto the LORD: for he hath torn, and he will heal us; he hath smitten, and he will bind us up. . . . Then shall we know . . . the LORD" (Hos. 6:1, 3) The Church could never fit into this framework of developments in the Tribulation.

The purpose test. Since purpose is primary with Deity, what precisely is the purpose of the tribulation judgments? In brief, it is twofold. First, to purge out the Jewish rebels: "I will cause you to pass under the rod, . . . And I will purge out from among you the rebels, and them that transgress against me: . . . and they shall not enter into the land of Israel . . ." (Ezek. 20:37, 38). And, second, to punish Gentile rejectors: "And I will execute vengeance in anger and fury upon the heathen [Gentiles] such as they have not heard" (Mic. 5:15). "When the Lord shall have washed away the filth of the daughters of Zion [the Jewish side], and shall have purged the blood of Jerusalem from the midst thereof . . . [Gentile angle] . . ." (Isa. 4:4).

Now, lay this test alongside the plans of the Lord for the Church, and simply ask your own heart the simple question, Does the Church fit into this picture?

The propagation test. That the gospel shall be preached in the Tribulation is irrefutable. God has promised to make His Word available to all generations. When the Rapture takes all the true witnesses from the earth, the Lord will raise up and commission 144,000 servants to go forth (Rev. 7:3, 4). A servant of God is one who shows the way of salvation (Acts 16:17). These servants will preach the gospel of the kingdom. That they will preach to evangelize Gentiles as well as Jews is crystal clear, for after revealing their commission, John states that multitudes of "all nations, and kindreds, and people . . . washed their robes, and made them white in the blood of the Lamb" (Rev. 7:9, 14).

The presentation of the tribulation gospelers will be a rerun of John the Baptist's message; namely, "Repent, for the Kingdom is at hand." Thus, the propagation test would seem to obviate the likelihood of the Church's disseminating the gospel of the grace of God in that period.

The perseverence test. Note the appeal articulated by the tribulation preachers: "But he that shall endure unto the end, the same shall be saved" (Matt. 24:13; Mark 13:13). Is this the evangelistic exhortation today? If the Church will be operating in the Tribulation, as some believe, will its message change? Or will there be two types of gospel being preached? If such could be conceivable, what would be the situation if both Jews and Gentiles and Christians were in the same audience?

It seems so much more reasonable to believe that the

Lord, Who doeth all things decently and in order, would terminate one emphasis before authorizing and instituting another—especially one of a conflicting nature. This we are persuaded He will do.

The judgment test. When the Lord returns to this earth to sit on the throne of His glory, it is clearly stated that the Gentiles shall be gathered before Him, that He shall separate them one from another as a shepherd divides his sheep from the goats (Matt. 25:32, 33). However, there is nothing said here about the Judgment Seat of Christ when He comes. Yet, if the Church is here right through this same wrath period through which the nations shall go, when is the Church to be judged for its works? Would not an understanding of the ranks of the resurrection (see 1 Cor. 15:22, 23) put this matter into its proper perspective?

The context test. By "context" is meant that immediate area in the Scriptures where a particular matter is mentioned. In Matthew, Mark and Luke, where Jesus speaks of the Tribulation, He refers to the preaching of the gospel of the Kingdom, of being beaten in the synagogues and of enduring to the end to be saved. Such terminology is so obviously foreign to the gospel-of-grace structure that comment is rendered superfluous. How necessary it is to "rightly divide the word of truth."

While there are allusions to the period of universal judgment, or the Tribulation, in a number of later New Testament books, especially 1 and 2 Thessalonians, we must agree that the concentration of this truth is in Revelation 4 to 18, where the entries are prolific. In such contexts, Israel and the nations (Gentiles) are repeatedly mentioned, but the Church is conspicuously absent (not even mentioned).

The testimony test. In the realm of profession, who bears the testimony in that period? "And the dragon was wroth with the woman [Israel], and went to make war with the remnant of her seed, which keep the commandments of God, and have the testimony of Jesus Christ" (Rev. 12:17). This is most revealing.

Who, then, will do the preaching in the Tribulation? The sealed or divinely commissioned servants who will be "of all the tribes of the children of Israel" (Rev. 7:4) and the "two witnesses" (Rev. 11:3). If the Church were there, what precisely would it be preaching when the gospel of the Kingdom is everywhere being declared, and when the hearts of the Jewish people are being turned to the fathers, to Israel's cherished antecedents (Mal. 4:6)?

Further, "And when the dragon saw that he was cast unto the earth [and he won't be cast down till the Church is caught up], he persecuted the woman [Israel] which brought forth the man child . . . and went to make war with the remnant of her seed . . ." (Rev. 12:13, 17). If the Church goes into that period, how can we account for the fact that nothing is said about the dragon [Satan] spewing out the venom of his animosity against her for bearing a witness for Christ? Observe carefully, "For as a snare shall it [the judgment of God] come on *all* them that dwell on the face of the *whole earth*" (Luke 21:35, *emphasis mine*). Yet, where do we read of the Church being persecuted? And why not, if Israel will be persecuted for the testimony of Christ?

The expectancy test. When the apostle Paul tells us about ". . . the grace of God . . . , teaching us that, denying ungodliness and worldly lusts, we should live soberly, righteously, and godly, in this present world; looking for that blessed hope, and the glorious appearing of the great God and our Saviour Jesus Christ" (Titus 2:11-13), you will notice that the participle *looking* ties expectancy in with this present age. It is clear that constant watchfulness is emphasized. Indeed, it has a holy influence upon the life, for an any-moment expectancy should produce an every-moment readiness. And this is the divine exhortation! If we are to expect the Antichrist for seven years before the Lord Jesus comes, how could expectancy of His return be tied in with this present age? And what would this do to the "blessed hope" concept?

The whole character of the situation, when put into proper perspective, indicates definitely that the Church, the Body of Christ, will not be there. We cannot, for instance, reconcile being killed by Antichrist and being kept by the Lord; or being overcome by the beast and being overshadowed by the Almighty, especially when there is no information in that regard.

In his book, *The Church Will Go Through the Tribulation,* author Jim McKeever advances copious instructions and suggestions for God's people to prepare for the indescribable experience of living under the Antichrist. In brief, this is the gist of his appeal:

1. Provide for a fallout shelter.
2. Store a supply of water.
3. Stock dehydrated foodstuffs.
4. Arrange bulk storage for staples.
5. Acquire earthquake information.
6. Move to a self-supporting area (rural).
7. Provide solar energy.

The author terms these measures "practical suggestions for preparation." Notwithstanding the author's unquestionable sincerity and compassion, could anything be more impractical? Since we do not know when the Tribulation will commence, when do believers begin this impossible task? The elderly, the handicapped, the bedridden and the poor would find all of this far beyond the pale of possibility.

Since this fantastic suggested preparation could not be made by the multitudes in condominiums and high-rise apartments, or in the average city-dweller's small home, where could they find "self-supporting" areas? Can one imagine such an attempted exodus? Who would organize it? What percentage of the Christian community could be convinced that this is a part of spiritual wisdom? Is it consonant with an upward look to go underground in shelters? Even though the "end time" is upon us, and unmistakably far advanced, have any begun as of this point in time to make such drastic and unreasonable "preparation"? It seems no less foolish than the hysteria the cultists create in summoning their people to the top of some mountain to prepare for "the end of the world."

Where in the Scriptures is there the slightest intimation of such a procedure as this? Since our posttribulationist friends insist upon building much of their position in the Gospel of Matthew (the sixty-ninth week of Daniel) before the Church was constituted as the Body of Christ, would it not be more consistent for them to sound out vociferously, "... Take no thought for your life, what ye shall eat, or what ye shall drink; nor yet for your body, what ye shall put on ..." (Matt. 6:25)?

How much foodstuff would be required for seven horrendous years of the Tribulation? How could it be protected from the lawless hordes crying for bread? How could water be stored in such vast quantities for such vast numbers for such a long period of time? Since harnessing the solar rays is beyond the reach of the rank and file, how could believers develop sufficient energy from this source? Where would they obtain the electricity and the gasoline required when they cannot buy without the mark of the beast? These are but a few of the many questions which surface at such a suggestion.

Then, too, does not this make the emphasis materialistic when, in the context of the above quotation, the Lord says, "But seek ye first the kingdom of God, and his righteousness; and all these things shall be added unto you" (Matt. 6:33)?

When people attempt to place the Church in an unrelated context, these are some of the problems which arise to confuse, disturb and frustrate those who should be rejoicing in the soon coming of our Lord—the real "blessed hope" of the true believer.

The Summary

A recapitulation of the salient facts of this treatise may help to crystalize the matter as we so thoroughly believe the Scriptures present it:

1. Trials and afflictions which have plagued believers along their pilgrim journey, either in antiquity or in contemporary times, cannot be equated with the tribulation developments, for Jesus clearly stated, "For then shall be great tribulation, such as was not since the beginning of the world to this time, no, nor ever shall be" (Matt. 24:21).

2. The period which concerns us is part and parcel of the seventy weeks of years God determined upon Daniel's people and upon their holy city (Dan. 9:24), and the Church is no more involved in the seventieth week than was the Church involved in the preceeding sixty-nine weeks. As we cannot put the Church back in the sixty-ninth week, just so we cannot place it over in the seventieth week.

3. God, Who does all things decently and in order, will certainly conclude His dealings with the Church before He resumes His dealings with Israel.

4. The Church will be "caught up" before the Tribulation because...
   a. The seventieth week of Daniel then begins, and it is not determined upon the Church any more than were the preceding sixty-nine weeks.
   b. We (believers) are saved from "the wrath to come" (1 Thess. 1:10).
   c. The Church is nowhere mentioned in the whole tribulation context of Revelation 4—18.
   d. References are made to Antichrist dealing with Israel in that period, but never to his dealings with the Church.
   e. Israel will have "the testimony of Jesus Christ" in the Tribulation (Rev. 12:17), but there is no mention of the Church sharing it with them.
   f. Antichrist will persecute Israel for her Christian witness, but there is no intimation of his persecuting the Church.
   g. God will reserve a place of protection and will nourish the believing Jews (Rev. 12:14), but such a provision is nowhere hinted for the Church.
   h. For *ALL* on the face of the earth it will be either the mark of the beast and doom, or refusal and death. Thus, the Church couldn't be around very long if God means what He says—*ALL*.
   i. Without the mark of the beast, which a Christian surely would not take, there can be neither buying nor selling. Thus, no human being could live more than days without food, much less for years.
   j. The chief purposes of the period being considered are (1) to purge out the rebels from Israel so they will not enter the kingdom (Ezek. 20:38); and (2) to judge the nations (Mic. 5:15). The Church is not included in these intended purposes.
   k. Throughout the Old Testament there are prolific references to the Tribulation, but not one reference is for the Church because the Church is not seen in Old Testament Scriptures (Eph. 3:5). Actually, the same would be true in the gospel records since the "law period" did not

end until Christ was crucified. "For Christ is the end of the law for righteousness to everyone that believeth" (Rom. 10:4).

l. The Matthew 24 context is not applicable to the Church because (1) the Body of Christ was not yet formed (Col. 1:18); (2) the message of enduring to the end to be saved is not compatible with the gospel of grace for the Church Age (Eph. 2:8); and (3) all the features of 1 Thessalonians 4:13—18 are in definite contrast with Matthew 24.

m. By statement and symbol, by figure and fact, the Church is not discoverable in the seventieth week of Daniel or the Tribulation.

If we believe that the fulness of divine wrath was poured out on Christ as believers' Substitute at Calvary, then we must believe that God will not pour out His wrath on us. We believe He saves all the way. The "blessed hope" of His appearing to receive us unto Himself is our greatest comfort and encouragement as the days grow ominously darker.

> O earth, what sorrow lies before thee,
>   Unlike it in the ages past;
> The fiercest throes that ever tore thee,
>   E'en though the briefest and the last.
>
> I see the shadows of the sunset;
>   I see the dread avenger's form;
> I see Armageddon's onset,
>   But I shall be above the storm.
>
> I hear the moaning and the sighing
>   I see the hot tears bitter fall—
> A thousand agonies of dying,
>   But I shall be above them all.
>   — Author unknown

"Thanks be to God, which giveth us the victory through our Lord Jesus Christ" (1 Cor. 15:57).